A Newbies Guide to Using

GarageBand

For the iPad

Minute Help Guides

Minute Help Press
www.minutehelp.com

Table of Contents

CHAPTER 1: WHAT YOU NEED TO KNOW 3

    THE CONTROL BAR 3

CHAPTER 2: THE BASICS 5

    KEYBOARD 5

    DRUMS 12

    GUITAR AMP 15

    AUDIO RECORDER 20

    SAMPLER 22

    SMART DRUMS 25

    SMART STRINGS 27

    SMART BASS 33

    SMART KEYBOARD 36

    SMART GUITAR 40

CHAPTER 3: ADVANCED TECHNIQUES 43

    RECORDING AND EDITING INSTRUMENTS 43

    EDITING A SONG 52

    ADDING APPLE LOOPS 57

    BUILDING A SONG WITH SONG SECTIONS 59

    JAM SESSION 62

CHAPTER 4: SYNCING, IMPORTING AND EXPORTING 64

    TO USE iCLOUD 64

    TO SHARE A SONG USING iTUNES 68

    TO IMPORT A SONG USING iTUNES 69

    TO IMPORT AN AUDIO FILE 70

CHAPTER 5: CONCLUSION 71

ABOUT MINUTE HELP PRESS 72

Chapter 1: What you need to know

GarageBand for iPad is simply a remarkable app. It's virtually a showcase for what the technology and design wizards at Apple can do with a touchscreen. Part of its greatness is the way it uses the touchscreen to almost make it feel like you are playing various instruments. The other part is how it packs a sophisticated recording studio onto the supremely portable iPad.

If you've used GarageBand for Mac, you'll see a lot here that you'll be very familiar with. In the "Advanced Techniques" section, we'll talk about Track view, which is very much the same as the way you record music on the Mac (if you haven't, don't worry; we'll cover it all). However, the software instruments we just mentioned are pretty unique – not just to the GarageBand app, but anywhere. That's the part we'll cover first, in "The Basics"

GarageBand for iPad is so sophisticated that you can actually create a song by ear, with virtually no knowledge of music theory. Still, however, music theory is part of songwriting, and terms from music theory apply to various GarageBand features and controls. We'll italicize some important music theory terms such as *key*, *tempo*, *meter* and *pitch* – as well as recording terms such as *track* or *playhead*. If you see anything you're unfamiliar with, there are many sources online that offer free introductions to music theory. If you'd prefer to learn more right on your iPad, there are several music theory apps available as well.

Along with italicizing some music terms, we'll boldface key parts of the interface that you'll interact with – like the **Navigation button** and the **Control bar**.

The Control Bar

The **Control bar** appears at the top of most of software instrument screens, and every Track view screen. These are the controls that you will see on the **Control bar** from right to left:

My Songs button – displays a drop down menu you can use to load a new song.

Instruments button – choose a new instrument.

Undo button – this button only appears after you have recorded an instrumental track. We'll cover recording tracks in the "Advanced Techniques" section.

View buttons – there are two **View buttons** that you can use to switch between Instrument view and Track view for every track in your song. We'll cover making songs in the "Advanced Techniques" section.

Go to Beginning button – like on a CD player, this moves playback back to the beginning of the song. While the song is playing, the **Go to Beginning button** turns into the **Stop button**.

Play button – starts playing the song. If a song is already playing, this stops it, leaving the playhead right where it is.

Record button – begins recording. To stop recording, but remain at that exact place, tap the **Play button** instead of the **Stop button**.

Master Volume slider – this controls the overall volume of the song.

Jam Session button – opens the Jam Session screen.

Controls button – opens or closes the controls area for the current Instrument. The Controls button only appears in Instrument view.

Loop Browser button – opens the Loop Browser, where you can find prerecorded music loops to add to your song. The **Loop Browser button** only appears in Tracks view.

Mixer button – this opens the Mixer section where you can control such functions as individual track volume, panning to the right or left, and effects.

Settings button – offers options to change important information such as the song's key, tempo, etc. You can also access GarageBand Help through this menu.

Chapter 2: The Basics

The first time you launch GarageBand you'll see the Instruments screen. It will show the Keyboard icon. You can access other instruments by swiping to the right or left.

Keyboard

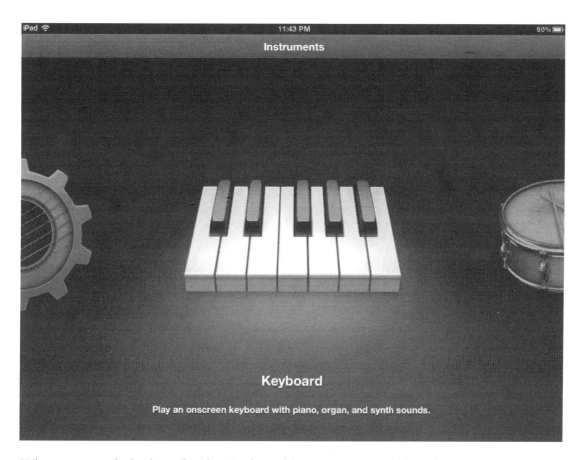

When you touch the icon for the Keyboard instrument, you'll be taken to the Keyboard screen. The default setting is Grand Piano. It will start at *Middle C* and show two octaves. Tapping any key is like striking a key on a piano. Tapping harder makes the sound somewhat louder, and holding the key down after you press it causes the note to continue, or *sustain*.

TIP: Try pressing the button just above the keyboard, with the keyboard icon, to see several layout options. You can chose layouts with fewer, larger keys for ease of play or more, smaller keys for parts that require a greater musical range.

To change the keyboard sound

Press the instrument icon in the upper right hand corner of the screen, just below the **Control bar**.

You'll see the Sound Chooser.

Use the buttons at the bottom to see several categories of available sounds. Note that each category has several pages of sounds to choose from.

To choose another sound, just tap the icon for that sound.

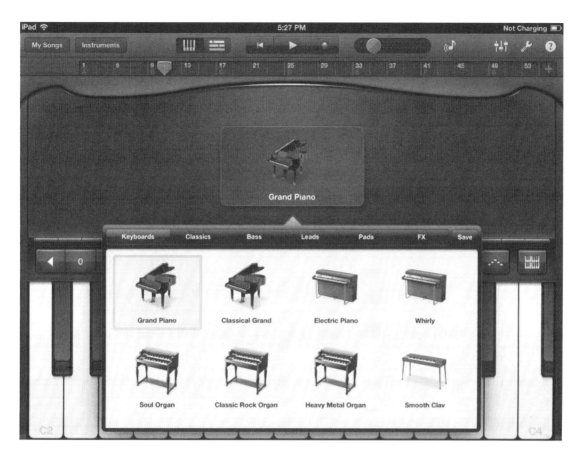

TIP: Note that the options listed about the keyboard will change, depending on what type of sound you choose.

To play higher or lower notes

To play higher or lower notes than those shown on screen, tap the **Octave Up** or **Octave Down** arrows above the keyboard, on the far left.

TIP: If you need one more note than what's shown on the screen, tapping just to the right of the far-right key or just to the left of the lowest key will sound one additional note.

To make a note hold longer

If you want to make the notes longer, or *sustain*, you can just by hold the key longer. However, to sustain a whole section of a song, tap and hold the **Sustain button** above the keyboard. If you slide the **Sustain button** to the left Sustain will lock on until you slide the button back to the right.

To adjust keyboard touch sensitivity:

The keys on the keyboard are touch sensitive – in other words, the notes will sound more loudly if you tap the keys harder. To adjust keyboard sensitivity, touch the **Settings button** in the upper right hand corner of the screen.

Select **Track Settings**.

Scroll down to Velocity Sensitivity.

Touch the current setting.

Select a new option from the Velocity Sensitivity screen.

*TIP: On most organ sounds, the **Sustain button** is replaced by a **Rotation switch**. This simulates the classic organ sounds of the classic '60s soul and rock.*

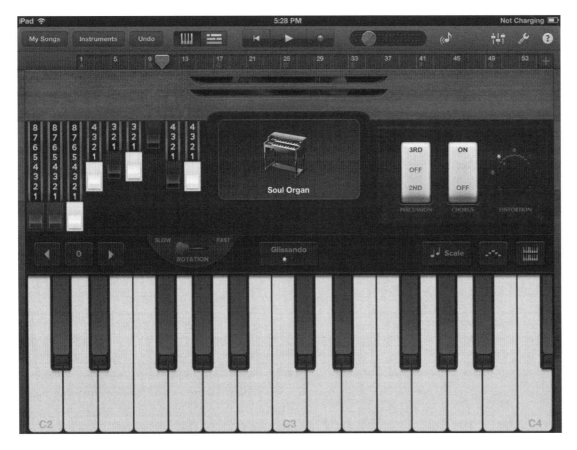

To adjust settings for swiping to the left or right:

The Grand Piano shows you a button above the keys, marked *Glissando*. If you swipe your finger from left to right the notes will play like dragging your finger across piano keys. You can change this setting to Scroll. On Scroll, dragging your finger to the right or the left moves the keyboard, showing additional keys to play.

On most synthesizers, you'll find a setting called **Pitch**. This bends the pitch to go up or down when you drag your finger.

To play only a selected scale

By applying a specific scale to the keyboard, you can make playing easier by eliminating notes you probably won't be using.

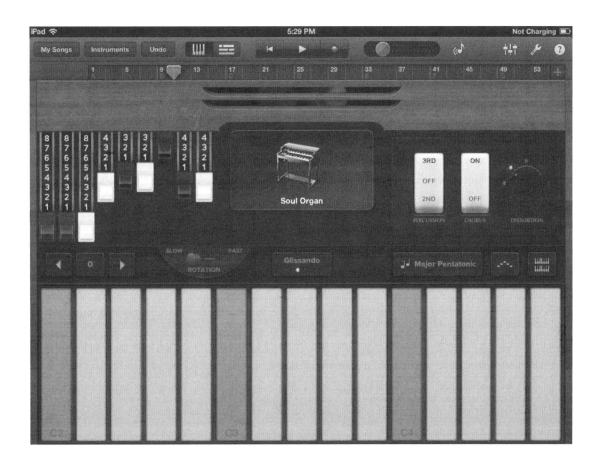

Drums

Much like the Keyboard, Drums will present you with a graphical interface that looks like a drum kit. As you might guess, you play the drum kit by tapping whichever percussion device that you want to sound. If you tap louder, the beat will sound more loudly as well.

Additionally, like real drums, the tone of the drum changes slightly on many of the instruments depending on whether you tap them near the center or near the edge. This can be helpful to add subtle variations.

TIP: Drum parts can get pretty intricate, pretty quickly. If you can't record your drum part properly all at once, try recording a basic beat and then add additional percussion, for more complex parts.

To change the drum sound

Press the button above the drum kit with the name of the current sound (such as **Classic Studio Kit**).

You'll see the Sound Chooser.

To choose another sound, just tap the icon for that sound.

To sync, or unsync, the bass drum and crash cymbal

In many drum arrangements, the bass drum and crash cymbal are struck at the same time. This is such a common approach that the default setting for drum kits sounds the crash cymbal every time the bass drum is tapped. To turn this off:

Touch the **Settings button** in the upper right-hand corner of the screen.

Turn **Bass drum with cymbal** to **Off**.

To adjust drum touch sensitivity

We already mentioned that the drums will sound more loudly if you tap the keys harder. To adjust drum sensitivity for your personal playing style:

Touch the **Settings button** in the upper right hand corner of the screen.

Select **Track Settings**.

Scroll down to Velocity Sensitivity.

Touch the current setting.

Select a new option from the Velocity Sensitivity screen.

Guitar Amp

The first two instruments we covered involved playing a virtual version of an actual instrument, using the touchscreen. The next group of instruments we'll look at allow you to capture sounds from outside of your iPad, to use in your songs.

In fact, the Guitar Amp looks and works a lot like a regular amp – it gives you a way to plug an electric guitar into your iPad.

To connect your guitar to your iPad

You will probably need to buy some type of third-party adaptor to connect your instrument to your iPad. There are several adapters you can find online, or at music and computer stores for anywhere from $30-$100 depending how fancy a device you want.

TIP: If you have an instrument, amp, or signal processing unit with a USB port, you can connect it to your iPad's data jack using Apple's Camera Connection Kit.

To change the guitar amp sound:

Touch the Guitar Amp screen.

Swipe your finger to the left or right.

There are three icons located in a row, below the **Control bar** and above the amp. They are Input, Tuner and Effects.

Input – Allows you to control input level. This also features a noise gate, to help reduce background noise. When an instrument is attached, you'll have a **Monitor switch**, to listen to your recording while you play.

Tuner – Helps you tune your instrument.

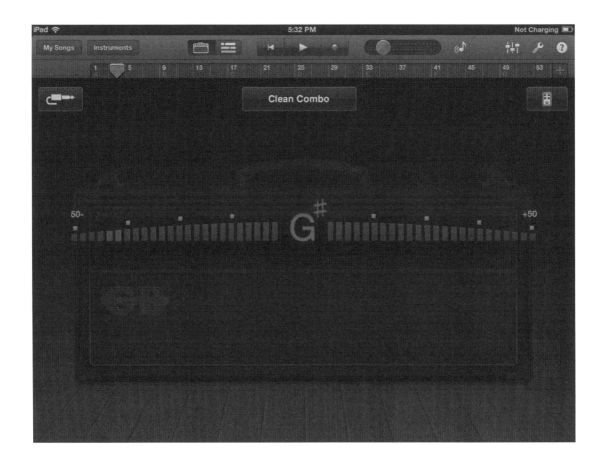

Effects – Allows you to apply popular guitar effects, such as distortion and echo.

To change the settings on the guitar amp controls

Touch the knob you want to change and slide you finger in a circle around that knob to change the settings.

Audio Recorder

GarageBand does a great job allowing you to record its own software instruments, but what about vocals? It would be impossible to bill your software as a recording studio without this key capability. Audio Recorder will allow you to capture your singing voice, acoustic instruments, or anything else you hear.

Like the Guitar Amp screen, the Audio Recorder features an Input icon, just below the **Control bar**, that works the exact same way.

To record with a microphone

To record using your iPad's built-in microphone, just tap the **Record button**.

You can also attach an external microphone to your iPad, see "Guitar Amp," above, for more information about finding adapters.

To add effects to a recording

After you complete your recording, several icons will appear on the screen. The icons allow you to add a variety of pre-set effects that can enhance your recordings. Tap any pre-set to select it.

Sampler

The Digital Sampler is a hybrid between a keyboard and the Audio Recorder. You can record small audio snippets using the iPad's built-in microphone, then you can play them back using the keyboard, allowing you to make any sound into a musical instrument.

To create a digital sample

When you first go to the Sampler screen, you will see a screen that is very much like the Audio Recorder. The methods of connecting devices and adjusting levels work the same, so please make sure you've looked at the Audio Recorder section above.

You record your sample by pressing the Start button at the bottom of the screen.

Use the Input Levels meter to make sure your recording is not too loud, or distortion will occur.

Press Stop when your recording is done

To playback digital samples

Press the **My Samples** button.

Choose a sample from the Library.

Press the **Controls button** on the **Control bar**. The Library will close, showing only a keyboard.

Play any key to trigger your sample.

To return to the Library, tap the **Controls button**.

To edit digital samples

Go to your Library and tap a sound to select it.

Tap the arrow next to the sample's name to go to the Sample Editor.

To edit the volume of different parts of your sample over time, tap **Shape**. Drag the points up or down to raise or lower the volume at that point.

To adjust the pitch, tap **Tune**. Use the **Coarse Tune** or **Fine Tune** sliders to make adjustments.

To trim the beginning or end of the sample, tap **Trim**. Drag the handles to the left or right.

To undo, tap **Revert**.

To play the sample backward, tap **Rev** (for Reverse).

To loop the sample, tap **Loop**.

Smart Drums

Smart Drums has a simple and unusual interface that makes it easy to create drum parts – however, you won't have absolute control as to how the part comes out.

When you go to Smart Drums, you'll see a square grid. Next to that grid, you'll see buttons for different percussion sounds.

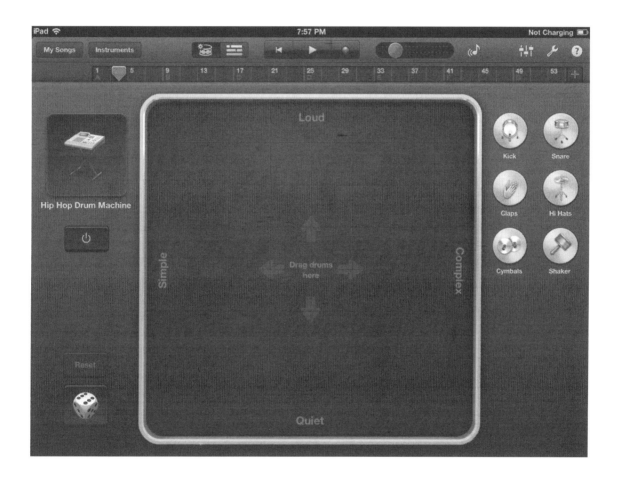

To hear the instrument associated with that button, simply touch a button. To add an instrument, just drag that button onto the grid. Drag it further towards the left for a simple part, or to the right for a more complex one. Drag it up for a louder sound, and down for a quieter volume.

TIP: If you want to get a better idea of how this works, just press the button on the lower left hand side of the screen that looks like dice. It will randomly generate a combination for you, and create another one every time you press the button.

To change the Smart Drum sound

Press the button on the left hand side of the screen with the picture of the current sound.

You'll see the Sound Chooser.

To choose another sound, just tap the icon for that sound.

Smart Strings

Smart Strings is another of Apple's smart instruments, and the first melodic smart instrument that we've looked at. A lot of the techniques that you'll learn in this section will also apply to Smart Bass, Smart Keyboard and Smart Guitar.

When you open Smart Strings, you'll see several strips that run vertically across the screen. At the top of each strip, you'll see the name of a chord. You can play these chord strips in two main ways.

Tap any strip to produce the sound of a string section all plucking the notes of that chord, called *pizzicato*.

To produce the sound of a string section playing more traditionally, with bows (called *legato*), run your finger up and down the strip in a bowing motion.

The notes will sustain as long as you keep moving your finger.

To change the string sound

In the upper left hand corner of the screen, touch the name of the current instrument sound (such as **Cinematic**).

To choose another sound, just tap the icon for that sound.

TIP: You'll find changing to different sounds in the Sound Chooser doesn't seem to change the sounds the strings make much at all. With Smart Strings, you'll only notice the big difference when you try out Autoplay, which we'll discuss in just a minute.

To play different string section sounds:

Smart String sections are comprised of several instrument sounds mixed together, just like a real string section. Options include 1st Violins, 2nd Violins, Violas, Cellos and Basses. By default, all of the sounds are turned on. If you want to alter the sound of your string section, try turning some off.

Above the chord strip, you'll see what looks like a stage, with an icon for every individual string sound.

When you touch an instrument, the icon fades, indicating you have turned off that sound. In the illustration below, we have turned off the Bass.

To use Autoplay:

Swipe your finger around the edge of the dial marked **Autoplay** to change it from Off to any one of the four numbered settings.

Touch the top of any of the chord strips to hear that chord played with the Autoplay setting you have chosen.

To play individual notes:

If you want to create a part by playing individual notes, change the **Chords/Notes** switch to Notes.

Select an instrument.

You will see a main screen that looks like the neck of a traditional stringed instrument.

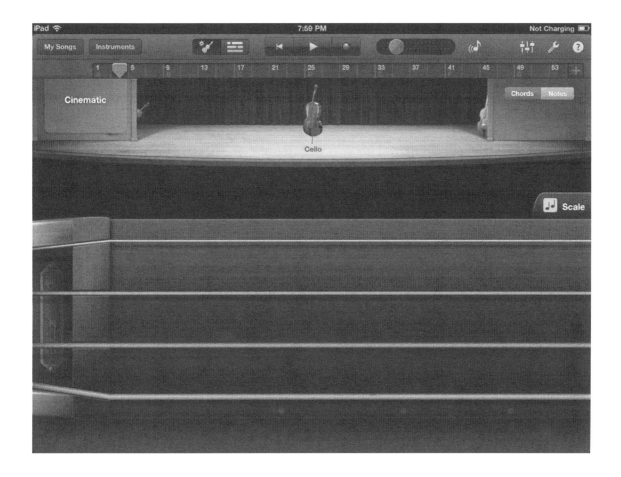

Touch any string to sound a note that would be produced by holding down that note and playing that string on the instrument.

TIP: *Remember, you can touch the **Scale tab** to choose a scale with appropriate notes for your music.*

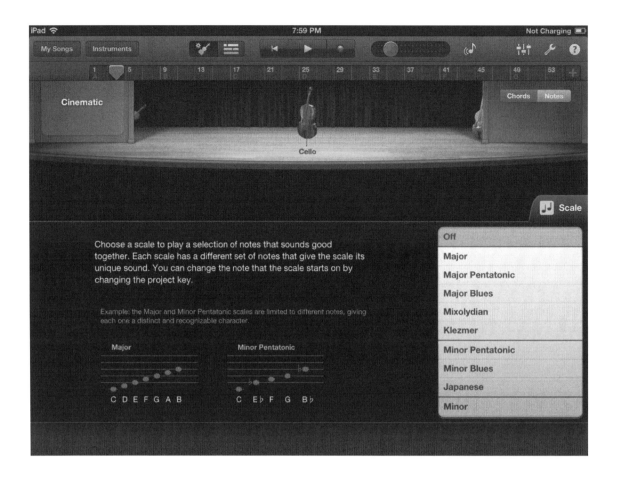

Smart Bass

You'll find many similarities between the Smart Bass screen and the Smart Strings, such as chord strips. Here, however, they work a little differently.

Each string is tuned to play one note from the chord that is named at the top of the strip. To produce a note, just tap that string, within the strip. By alternating strings within that strip, you'll be playing a bass part for that chord.

To change the bass sound:

In the upper left hand corner of the screen, touch the name of the current instrument sound (such as **Liverpool**).

You'll see the Sound Chooser.

To choose another sound, just tap the icon for that sound.

TIP: Although the icons for "synth bass" sounds look like keyboards, they're all played the same way.

To use Autoplay:

You can use Autoplay to make Smart Bass play bass grooves in various rhythms and styles.

In the upper right hand corner of the screen, swipe your finger around the edge of the dial marked **Autoplay** to change it from Off to any one of the four numbered settings.

Touch the top of any of the chord strips visible at the bottom of the screen to hear that chord played with the Autoplay setting you have chosen.

To play individual notes:

In the upper right hand side of the screen, change the **Chords/Notes** switch to Notes.

You will see a main screen that looks like the neck of a traditional bass.

Touch any string to sound a note that would be produced by holding down that note and playing that string on the instrument.

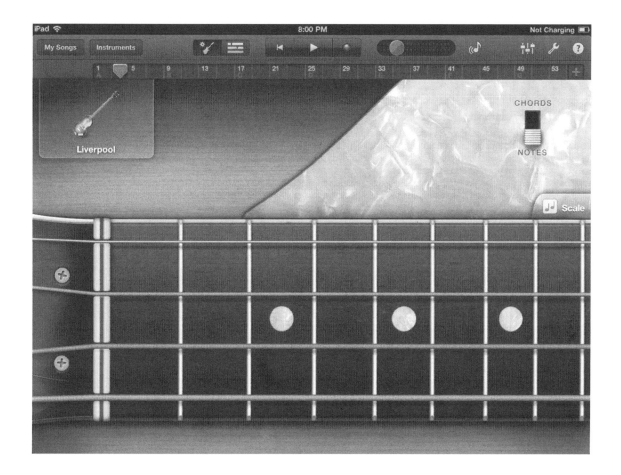

TIP: Like any of the smart melodic instruments, keep in mind that you have the option to use the **Scale tab**.

Smart Keyboard

Since you've already seen Keyboard, and you know how smart instruments work, you can probably make some educated guesses as soon as you see the Smart Keyboard. They even look similar, except that the keys of the Keyboard are replaced by the now-familiar chord strips. These chord strips work a little differently.

To play a full chord, tap the top of the chord strip (where the chord name is).

To play the chord as a series of notes (an *arpeggio*), run your finger up or down a chord strip.

To just play a bass note, touch one of the lower, shaded portions of the strip.

To play a smaller chord (like the right hand of a pianist would do), press anywhere in the upper, light grey portion of each strip.

To play the chord as a series of notes (an arpeggio), run your finger up or down a chord strip.

TIP: You can easily play a simple keyboard part by alternately tapping the lower and upper portions of the chord strip.

*TIP: The **Sustain button** (or, on organs, the **Rotation switch**) moves to the right hand side of the keyboard.*

To change the Smart Keyboard sound:

Press the **Navigation button**.

In the upper right hand corner of the screen, touch the name of the current instrument sound (such as **Grand Piano**).

You'll see the Sound Chooser.

To choose another sound, just tap the icon for that sound.

To use Autoplay

Swipe your finger around the edge of the dial marked **Autoplay** to change it from Off to any one of the four numbered settings.

Tap a portion of one of the chord strips.

The upper portions (showing the chord names) play chords and bass notes together.

The middle portions play only chords.

The lower portions play bass notes.

To return to using the regular chord strip, turn off Autoplay.

Smart Guitar

Again, you'll recognize a lot of similarities to other smart instruments, particularly Smart Bass:

To play chords, tap at the top of the chord strip, where the chord name is.

To strum the chord, set your finger down on a strip and slide it up or down.

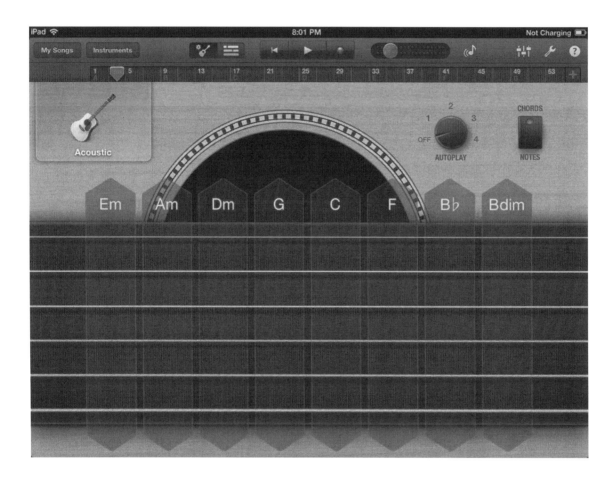

To change the Smart Guitar sound:

In the upper right hand corner of the screen, touch the name of the current instrument sound (such as **Acoustic**).

You'll see the Sound Chooser.

Use the buttons at the bottom to see several categories of available sounds. Note that each category has several pages of sounds to choose from.

To choose another sound, just tap the icon for that sound.

To use Autoplay:

Swipe your finger around the edge of the dial marked **Autoplay** to change it from Off to any one of the four numbered settings.

TIP: Notice that the electric guitar sounds also have effects you can use to customize the sounds.

To play individual notes:

In the upper right hand side of the screen, change the Chords/Notes switch to Notes.

You will see a main screen that looks like the neck of a traditional guitar.

Touch any string to sound a note that would be produced by holding down that note and playing that string on the instrument.

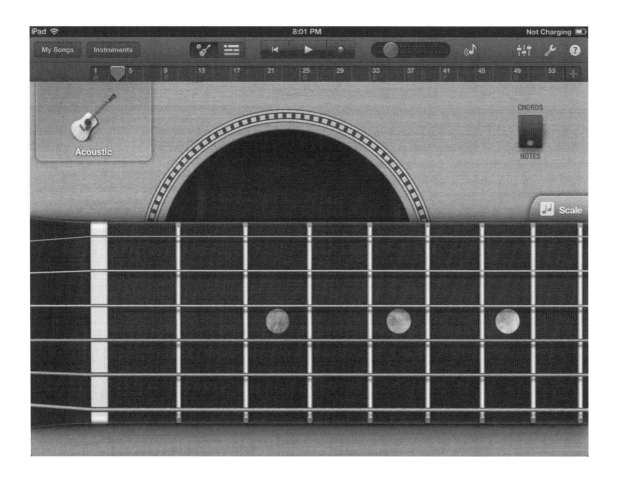

Chapter 3: Advanced Techniques

In a recording studio, each separate section of audio records a specific instrument (or group of instruments). The same is true in GarageBand, and you will combine these tracks to make a song. You can also add prerecorded snippets of music called Loops to enhance your songs, or to make an entire song, without even playing an instrument.

Recording and editing instruments

We've already discussed how to play the instruments. When you record any instrument, you're creating a track.

To record an instrument:

Tap the **Record button** in the middle section of the **Control bar**.

The ruler shows the region being recorded. Your recording will start where the *playhead* is.

Play the instrument.

Press the **Play button** to leave record mode.

*TIP: Hitting **Record** again usually records over the current part. For Drums, however, you can layer the parts by recording again, to create more complex parts.*

To edit the instrument recording you just made

Touch part of the recorded region on the Ruler, and slide your finger down. You will see the region displayed, just as you would see it in Tracks view.

Tap the region to select it.

Tap the region again to call up the Edit menu.

TIP: When you go into editing mode, the instrument portion of the screen dims to gray to indicate that you can't play the instrument until you're done editing.

To switch to another recorded instrument, tap the instrument icon to the left of the region and slide your finger up or down.

Also, as you record more regions, to build a song, you can skip from one region to another by touching the region and swiping your finger to the right or left.

*TIP: To make sure incoming phone calls, alerts and notifications don't interrupt you while recording, you can go into the Settings app and switch on **Airplane Mode**.*

Working with tracks

As you record instruments, you create tracks. Tracks can contain just part of an instrument – say the snare drum and bass drum of a drum part. They can contain an entire instrument, like the virtual guitar. Or you can merge several tracks if you're working on something really complex.

To move from Instrument view to Track view, just press the **Track View button** on the **Control bar**.

Use the **Ruler**, under the familiar **Control bar**, to measure where you are in the song by the measure.

Under that, you'll see a series of tracks. Each instrument has its own track. There is an icon to the left of every track, called the Track Header.

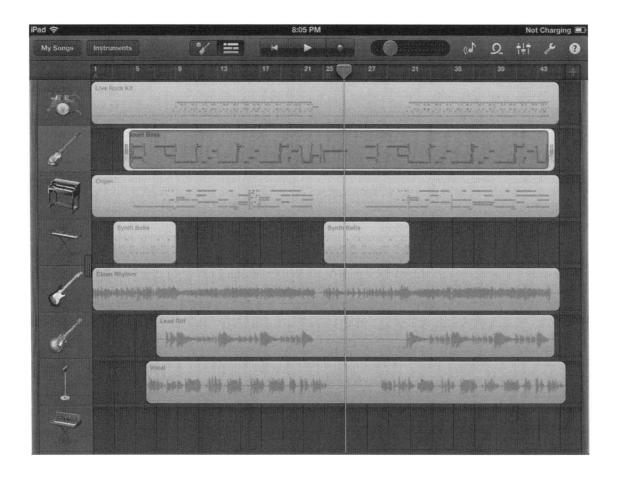

To show additional controls for each track

Touch the instrument icon to the left of any track – called the Track Header.

Slide it to the left.

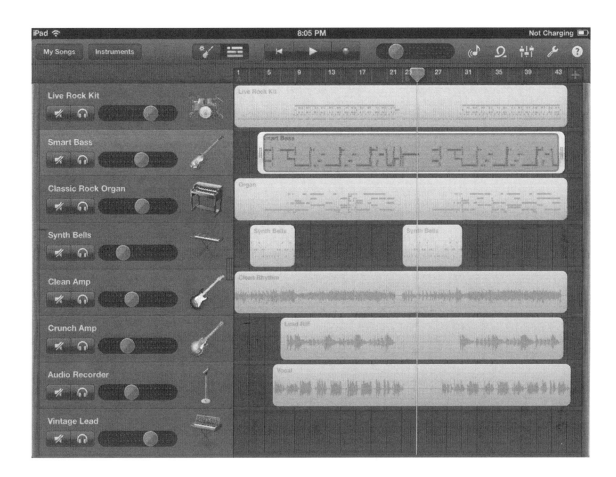

From right to left, the controls are – **Mute** (turns track off), **Solo** (only the selected track will play) and a **Volume slider**, which controls the volume of that track relative to all the others.

To close track controls, just slide any Track Header back to the left.

To change the order of tracks in Track view, touch and hold the Track Header for that track to select it, and slide your finger up or down to the new desired position.

To add a new track, scroll to the bottom of the Track view window and press the + **button**.

To edit the entire track, just select the track and then tap the Track Header. From the Edit menu, you can Delete the track or Merge it.

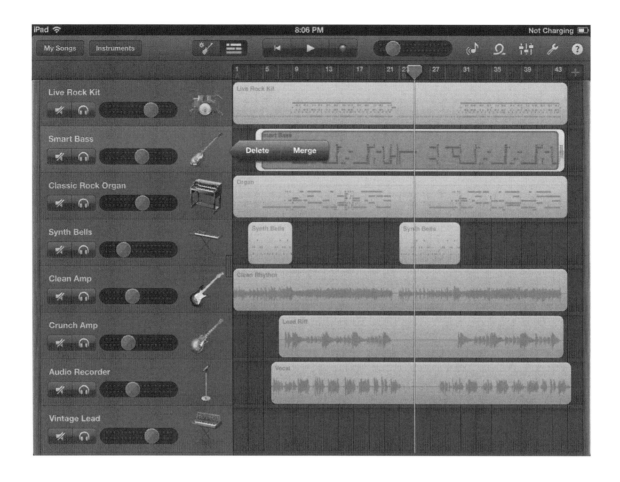

If you choose Merge, you will be prompted to select another track to merge with the currently selected track.

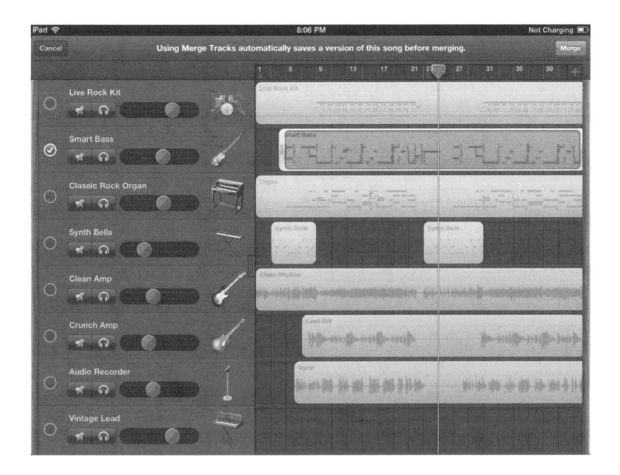

TIP: GarageBand only allows eight individual tracks, but you can make extra space by merging them.

To create a song

When you open GarageBand, the app creates a new song, titled "My Song."

When you record your first instrumental part, the song is saved.

To work with an already existing song

Tap the **Navigation button**

Tap **My Songs**

TIP: Going into the My Songs browser automatically saves the song you are currently working in. If you are working in a song and are making multiple changes, exit the song you are working in so GarageBand will save your work.

In the My Songs screen, tap the song you want to open.

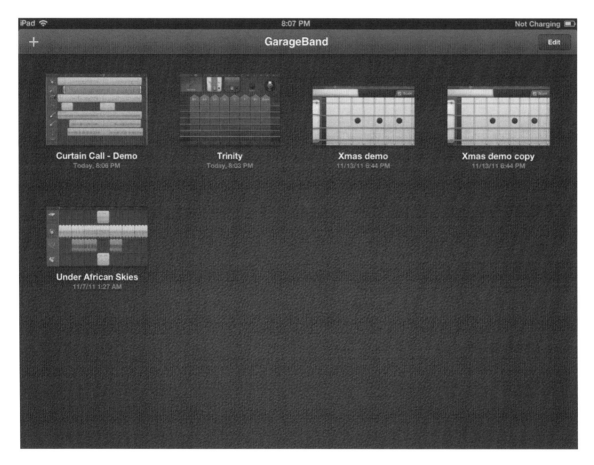

TIP: To create a new song, just tap the + button.

To create a song folder, touch and hold the icon for one song and drag it onto another.

To use Edit functions:

Tap the **Edit button** on the My Songs screen.

Tap the icon of the item you want to select.

Tap one of the icons in the upper left hand corner to share the song, Duplicate it or Delete it.

When finished, tap **Done**.

Editing a Song

We've already discussed tracks. Now, we're going to talk a bit about regions. If you record one instrument, that creates a track. Every time you start recording a segment and finish, that piece of music you just recorded is a region. When you're making a song, it helps to be able to add, move or delete regions. You can also edit individual notes inside the region itself.

To identify regions

There are three types of regions, identified by the colors blue, green or purple.

Blue regions are the prerecorded Apple Loops. We'll discuss Apple Loops in a minute.

Green regions are the software instruments you record.

Purple regions are audio regions from Audio Recorder or Guitar Amp.

To select regions

To select a region, just tap it.

To select multiple regions, touch and hold that region, and select additional regions by tapping them.

To select every region in a track, tap the Track Header.

To select every region, tap in an empty space in the Track view and then tap **Select All**.

To move a region, drag it to the right or left.

TIP: You can also drag a region up or down to another track, but only to another track with the same instrument.

To trim a region, select it, then touch the left or right edge of that region and drag it.

To loop a region, tap the region to select it. Tap it again and choose **Loop**.

To split a region, tap the region to select it. Tap it again and choose **Split**. Move the **Scissors icon** to where you want to split the region and slide the icon down.

To join two regions, touch and hold one region, while tapping another to select it. When you have selected all the regions you want, tap one and choose **Join**.

TIP: You can only join consecutive regions on the same track.

To copy, cut or paste a region, tap it to select it and tap it again to call up the Edit menu.

To undo your edit, just tap **Undo**.

To edit inside a region

You can only edit the green software regions you have recorded.

To open the editor

Tap a region to select it. Tap it again and choose **Edit**

Notes play from left to right across each bar. Higher pitched notes are placed on higher bars.

To select a note, tap it.

To select multiple notes, touch and hold one, and then tap additional notes.

Move notes to the right or left to adjust the timing.

Move notes up or down to change pitch.

Adding Apple Loops

Apple Loops offer plenty of prerecorded snippets that can be used to create a song, with very little knowledge of music theory. Or you can add them to a song you create. Apple Loops automatically adjust to the key and tempo of your songs.

To open the Loop Browser, press the Loop Browser button in Track view.

To find loops that will work with your song

Use any combination of the three buttons at the top of the screen to filter by Instrument, Genre and Descriptors (such as "Cheerful" or "Intense").

TIP: If you know the name of the loop you want, or even part, you can also use the Search box.

To hear what the loop sounds like, tap it. To stop the loop from playing, tap it again.

To add your loop to your song, touch and hold the icon for that loop and drag it to the right or left. You'll see the Track view. Drag the loop where you want it and let it go.

Building a Song with Song Sections

Most songs are made of several sections that repeat, like the *verse-chorus* structure of many popular songs. You can work more quickly by creating and using song sections. To open it tap the + **button** on the right-hand side of the **Ruler**.

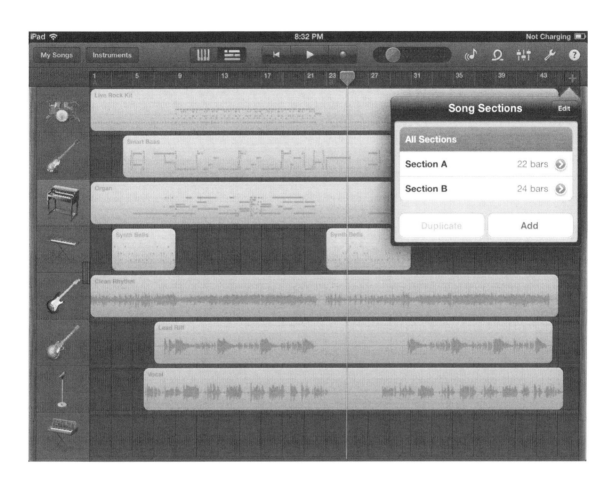

To add a song section

Tap the + **button**.

Tap **Add**.

Tap **Done**.

A section will be added to the end of the song.

To copy a section

Tap the + **button**.

Tap a section to select it.

Tap **Duplicate**.

Tap **Done**.

The duplicate will be added to the end of the song.

*TIP: You can also change the length of a section from this screen by touching the arrow next to the section's name, and using the **Up** and **Down** arrows in the Length of Section screen.*

To navigate to a different song section

Tap the + **button**.

Tap a section to select it.

Tap **Done**.

To play the entire song tap **All Sections**.

To move a section

Tap the + **button**.

Tap **Edit**.

Touch and hold the Handle icon on the right edge of the section you want to move.

Drag that section up or down to the desired location.

Tap **Done**.

The duplicate will be added to the end of the song.

To delete a section:

Tap the + **button**.

Tap **Edit**.

Tap the red circle on the left of the section you want to delete.

Tap **Done**.

Jam Session

Jam Session is an exciting new feature added to GarageBand. Using Jam Session, up to four musicians can play together in real time to create a song.

The person who starts the Jam Session is the bandleader. The bandleader chooses the basic song settings, such as key and tempo.

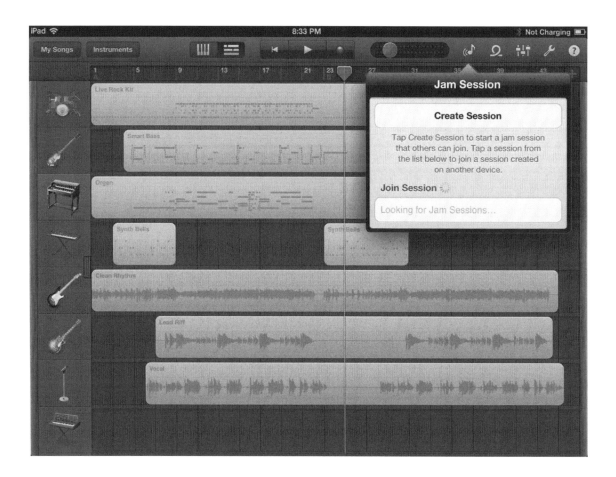

To access the Jam Session controls

Tap the Jam Session button on the **Control bar**.

Your iPad will automatically search for any available sessions.

To create a new Jam Session (and become the bandleader), tap **Create Session.**

To join a Jam Session as a band member, tap the name of the session you want to join.

By default, the bandleader controls the playback controls for the song. To share the ability, turn the **Bandleader Control** to Off.

To exit the Jam session, band members tap **Leave Session.**

To end the Jam Session, if you are the bandleader, tap **Stop Session**.

Chapter 4: Syncing, Importing and Exporting

Now, GarageBand has some great features for making music. But it also has some handy features that help you share your creation after it's done. GarageBand makes it easy to transfer your song to your Mac or share it online.

GarageBand also offers ways to import audio into your songs, so you can use these in other recordings.

To Use iCloud

You can use iCloud as an easy way to expand the power of GarageBand. If you have not already activated iCloud on your device, see Apple's instructions for doing so. Once you have activated iCloud, you can set GarageBand to use iCloud like so:

Tap the **Navigation button**.

Tap the **My Songs** button.

In the My Songs browser, tap the **Add Song** button.

Turn **Use iCloud** on.

To upload a song to iCloud:

Go to the **My Songs** browser.

Tap **Edit**.

Tap the name of the song you want to upload.

Tap the **iCloud button**.

Tap **Upload Song to iCloud**.

To download a song from iCloud

Go to the My Songs browser

Any song that is available in iCloud will show a small iCloud symbol in the corner of the song's icon.

Tap a song to download it.

To remove a song from iCloud:

Go to the My Songs browser.

Tap **Edit**.

Tap the song you want to remove.

Tap the **iCloud button**.

Tap **Remove Song from iCloud**.

TIP: You will still have a copy of your song on your iPad.

To share a song

Go to the My Songs browser.

Tap **Edit.**

Tap a song to select it.

Tap the **Share** button in the upper right hand corner.

You can share a song to Facebook, YouTube or SoundCloud if you have accounts with those services, just by logging in.

Additionally, if you have iMovie installed on your iPad, you can share with iMovie. The song will be added to the current iMovie project, or you can create a new project.

You can share a song to iTunes. See the next sections for details.

Finally, you can send the song by e-mail.

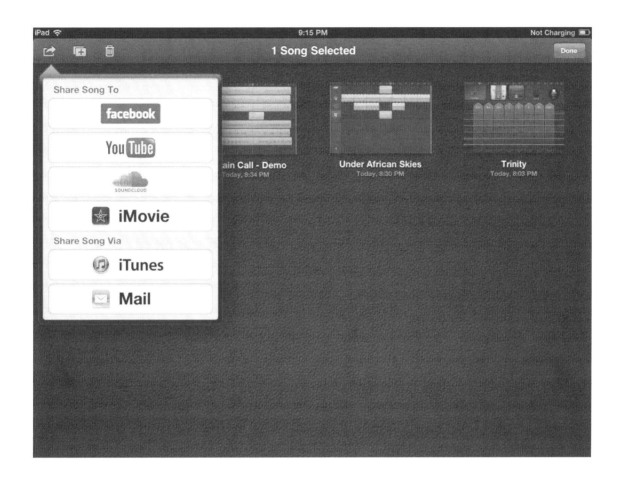

To Share a Song Using iTunes

There are two different ways to export your GarageBand project using iTunes. You can export it as a GarageBand file, if you would like to continue working with it. Or you can share it online.

TIP: You can export from your GarageBand for iPad to GarageBand for Mac, but it won't work the other way round.

To share a song with iTunes, follow the steps above and choose **Share Song via iTunes** and then follow these steps:

To share an audio file, tap iTunes.

Tap **Share**.

You'll be able to choose options to emphasize high audio quality, or smaller file size.

To share a GarageBand song, tap GarageBand.

Sync your iPad to your computer.

On your computer, go to **File Sharing in iTunes**.

Drag the file from the GarageBand Documents to the Finder.

To Import a Song Using iTunes

Connect your iPad to your computer.

Using iTunes on your computer, select **Apps**.

On the File Sharing Apps list, choose **GarageBand**.

Drag the GarageBand file you want to share onto the Documents list.

On your iPad, go to your My Songs browser.

Tap the **My Songs button**.

Tap the + **button**.

Select **Copy from iTunes**.

Tap the song you want to import.

To Import An Audio File

To import an audio file to use as part of a song you are creating, the process is a little different.

Follow the steps above, but drag an audio file into the Documents list.

Open a project in GarageBand on your iPad.

Go to Tracks view.

Select, or create, an audio (purple) track.

Open the Loop Browser.

Tap **Audio Files**.

Select the audio file you want to include.

TIP: You can import files in AIFF, WAV and MP3 formats.

Chapter 5: Conclusion

The wonderful thing about GarageBand for iPad is that there is no limit to what you can do. If you'd like to have fun and make some music, this app will help you do so.

But even if you are a more ambitious composer, GarageBand can be a useful part of your workflow. Artists such as Rhianna, Fred Durst (Limp Bizkit), Patrick Stump (Fall Out Boy), Erasure, Nine Inch Nails, Panic At The Disco!, Courtney Love, T-Pain, and Seal have used GarageBand to demo, record, and even release tracks for fans to remix.

We hope you enjoy using GarageBand for iPad to make music, and to share it with your friends and fans. Good luck!

About Minute Help Press

Minute Help Press is building a library of books for people with only minutes to spare. Follow @minutehelp on Twitter to receive the latest information about free and paid publications from Minute Help Press, or visit minutehelp.com

9528927R00043

Printed in Great Britain
by Amazon.co.uk, Ltd.,
Marston Gate.